PADDiNGTON 2

STUDiOCANAL

HEYDAY FILMS

WISE PUBLICATIONS
part of The Music Sales Group
London / New York / Paris / Sydney / Copenhagen /
Berlin / Madrid / Hong Kong / Tokyo

FOREWORD

It's hard for me not to have a soft spot for Paddington in my heart. Like me, he came to live in London from afar, and made it his home. He fell in love with this city long ago and can't help but see its beauty wherever he turns.

He bought into an ideal of British life that stands for decency, kindness, generosity and open-mindedness. His, of course, is an idealised London — one that exists mostly as an aspiration perhaps. But then again, what should one aspire to?

The music in the movie, and in this book, owes more than a little to the thought that Charlie Chaplin, Jacques Tati, Buster Keaton and Tommy Cooper (to mention but a few gentle and mishap-prone fellow comedians) would happily share a marmalade sandwich with the little bear. Paddington goes about life expecting the best of everyone, and because of this, he mostly gets it. As a mirror not of what reality is, but of what we wish it could be, as our guide to the direction we'd like to see the world moving in, he carries the flag.

Dario Marianelli

PADDINGTON THEME 5

THE POP-UP BOOK 6

A SHAVE, SIR? A LIGHT POMADE? 9

WINDOW CLEANING 12

THE BOOK IS STOLEN 17

KANGAROO COURT 22

A LETTER FROM PRISON 24

MADAME KOZLOVA'S STORY 26

WHAT ARE WE GOING TO DO? 29

JUNGLE JAIL 42

ESCAPE WALTZ 30

ASCENSION 34

EPILOGUE 36

THE POP-UP BOOK (PIANO DUET) 38

PADDINGTON THEME

MUSIC BY DARIO MARIANELLI

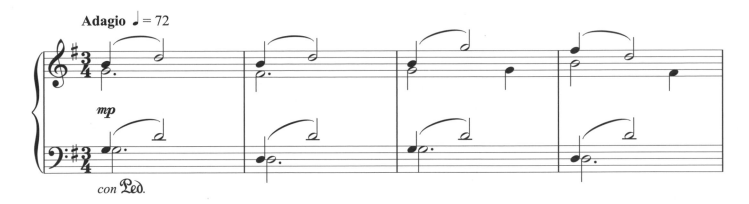

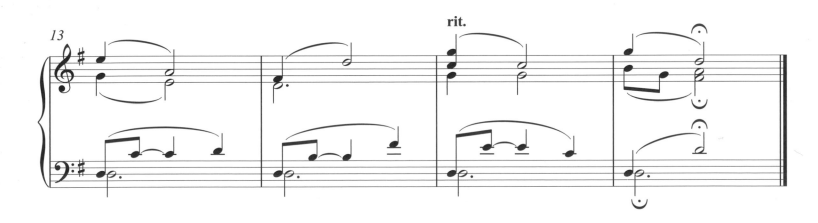

THE POP-UP BOOK

MUSIC BY DARIO MARIANELLI

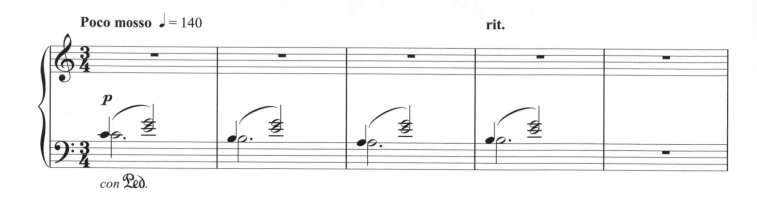

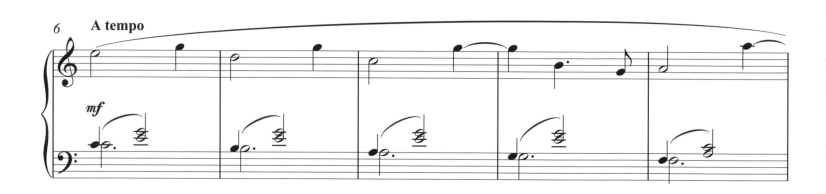

A SHAVE, SIR? A LIGHT POMADE?

MUSIC BY DARIO MARIANELLI

molto rall.   A tempo

WINDOW CLEANING

MUSIC BY DARIO MARIANELLI

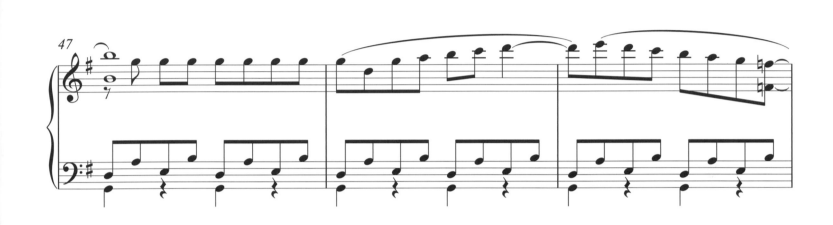

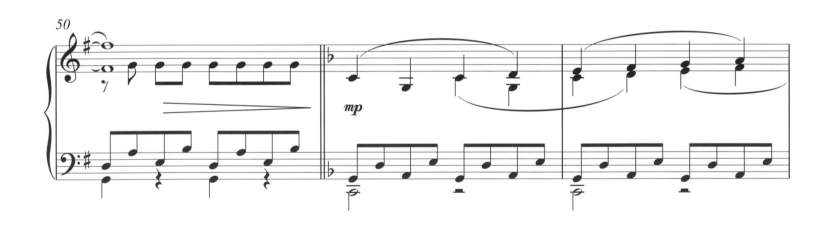

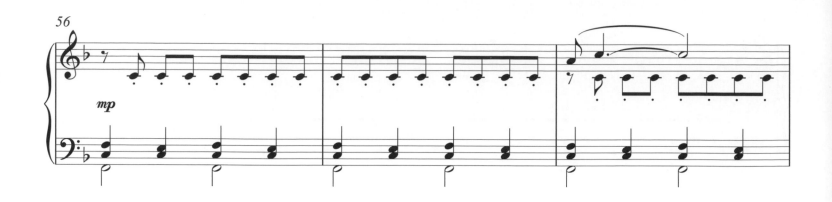

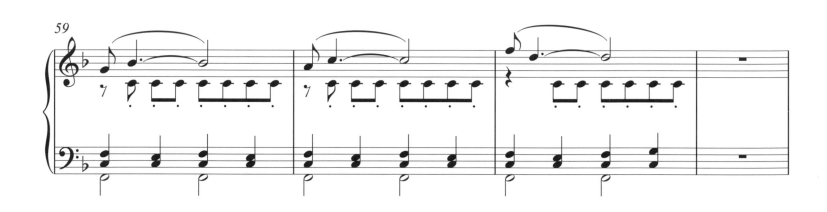

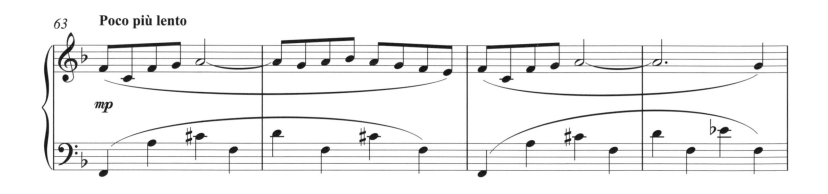

THE BOOK IS STOLEN

MUSIC BY DARIO MARIANELLI

KANGAROO COURT

MUSIC BY DARIO MARIANELLI

A LETTER FROM PRISON

MUSIC BY DARIO MARIANELLI

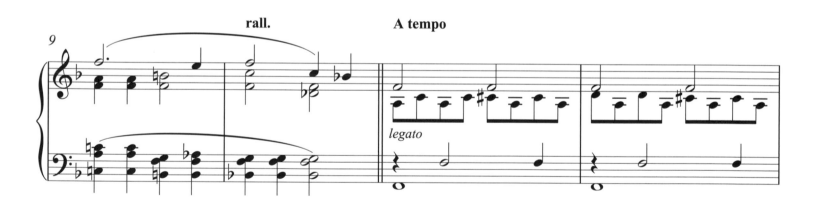

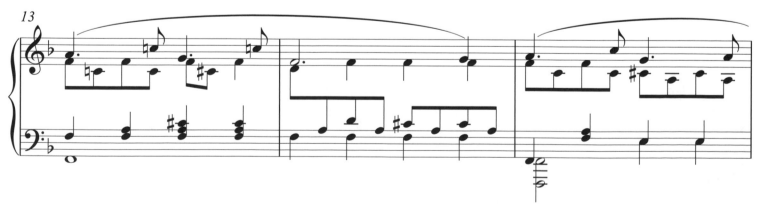

MADAME KOZLOVA'S STORY

MUSIC BY DARIO MARIANELLI

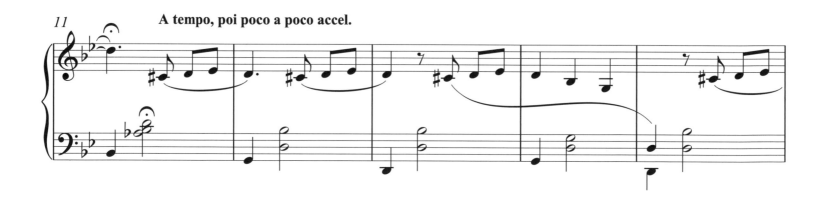

WHAT ARE WE GOING TO DO?

MUSIC BY DARIO MARIANELLI

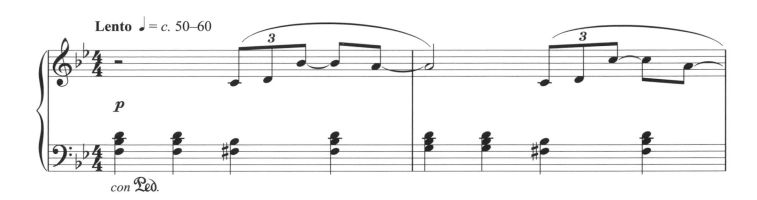

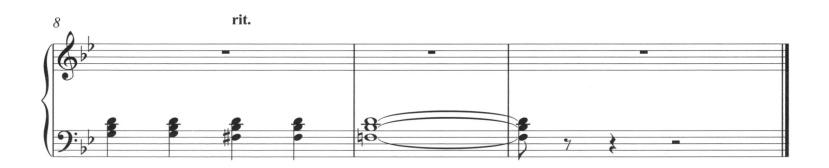

ESCAPE WALTZ

MUSIC BY DARIO MARIANELLI

ASCENSION

MUSIC BY DARIO MARIANELLI

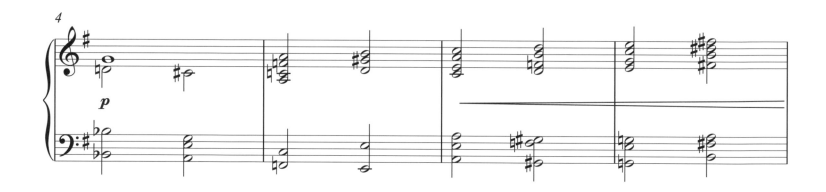

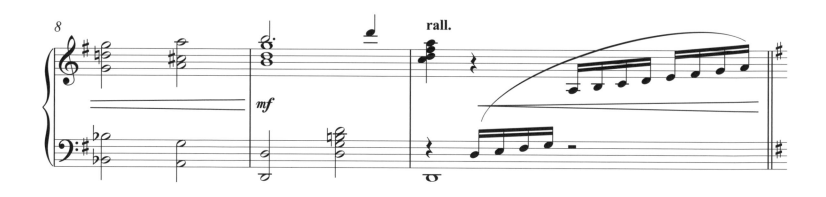

EPILOGUE

MUSIC BY DARIO MARIANELLI

THE POP-UP BOOK (PIANO DUET)

MUSIC BY DARIO MARIANELLI

SECONDO

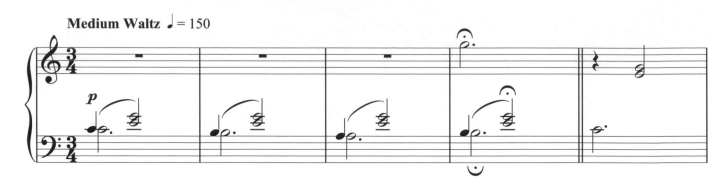

THE POP-UP BOOK (PIANO DUET)

MUSIC BY DARIO MARIANELLI

PRIMO

JUNGLE JAIL

MUSIC BY DARIO MARIANELLI

44

Published by
WISE PUBLICATIONS
14-15 Berners Street, London W1T 3LJ, UK.

Exclusive Distributors:
MUSIC SALES LIMITED
Distribution Centre, Newmarket Road, Bury St Edmunds, Suffolk IP33 3YB, UK.

MUSIC SALES CORPORATION
180 Madison Avenue, 24th Floor, New York NY 10016, USA.

MUSIC SALES PTY LIMITED
4th floor, Lisgar House, 30-32 Carrington Street, Sydney, NSW 2000, Australia.

Order No. AM1013727
ISBN: 978-1-78760-031-7
This book © Copyright 2018 Wise Publications,
a division of Music Sales Limited.

Unauthorised reproduction of any part of this publication
by any means including photocopying is an infringement of copyright.

Original music by Dario Marianelli.
Edited by James Welland.
Additional arrangements by Alistair Watson.
Music processed by Sarah Lofthouse, SEL Music Art Ltd.
Original score published by Studiocanal S.A.S.
Original design and images courtesy of Studiocanal.
Additional design by Tim Field.

Printed in the EU.

UNITED STATES:

WARNER BROS. PICTURES AND STUDIOCANAL PRESENT IN ASSOCIATION WITH ANTON CAPITAL ENTERTAINMENT S.C.A. A HEYDAY FILMS PRODUCTION "PADDINGTON 2" HUGH BONNEVILLE SALLY HAWKINS BRENDAN GLEESON JULIE WALTERS JIM BROADBENT PETER CAPALDI WITH HUGH GRANT AND BEN WHISHAW AS THE VOICE OF PADDINGTON CASTING BY NINA GOLD AND LAUREN EVANS COSTUME DESIGNER LINDY HEMMING COMPOSER DARIO MARIANELLI EDITORS MARK EVERSON AND JONATHAN AMOS ACE PRODUCTION DESIGNER GARY WILLIAMSON DIRECTOR OF PHOTOGRAPHY ERIK ALEXANDER WILSON EXECUTIVE PRODUCERS ROSIE ALISON JEFFREY CLIFFORD ALEXANDRA FERGUSON DERBYSHIRE RON HALPERN DIDIER LUPFER 'PADDINGTON BEAR' CREATED BY MICHAEL BOND WRITTEN BY PAUL KING AND SIMON FARNABY PRODUCED BY DAVID HEYMAN DIRECTED BY PAUL KING

STUDIOCANAL   HEYDAY FILMS   ACE ANTON CAPITAL ENTERTAINMENT   WB   DOLBY

THE REST OF THE WORLD:

STUDIOCANAL PRESENTS IN ASSOCIATION WITH ANTON CAPITAL ENTERTAINMENT S.C.A. WITH THE PARTICIPATION OF CANAL+ CINE+ AND AMAZON PRIME INSTANT VIDEO A HEYDAY FILMS PRODUCTION "PADDINGTON 2" HUGH BONNEVILLE SALLY HAWKINS BRENDAN GLEESON JULIE WALTERS JIM BROADBENT PETER CAPALDI WITH HUGH GRANT AND BEN WHISHAW AS THE VOICE OF PADDINGTON CASTING BY NINA GOLD AND LAUREN EVANS COSTUME DESIGNER LINDY HEMMING COMPOSER DARIO MARIANELLI EDITORS MARK EVERSON AND JONATHAN AMOS ACE PRODUCTION DESIGNER GARY WILLIAMSON DIRECTOR OF PHOTOGRAPHY ERIK ALEXANDER WILSON EXECUTIVE PRODUCERS ROSIE ALISON JEFFREY CLIFFORD ALEXANDRA FERGUSON DERBYSHIRE RON HALPERN DIDIER LUPFER 'PADDINGTON BEAR' CREATED BY MICHAEL BOND WRITTEN BY PAUL KING AND SIMON FARNABY PRODUCED BY DAVID HEYMAN DIRECTED BY PAUL KING

STUDIOCANAL   HEYDAY FILMS   ACE ANTON CAPITAL ENTERTAINMENT   amazon Prime Instant Video   CANAL+   CINE +   DOLBY